2

Would you rather...

be with a lover who is very adventurous in bed but is bad at sex

OR

be with a lover who is great at sex but is limited to only 1 style at sex?

3

Would you rather...

give your partner oral sex

OR

get oral sex from your partner?

How to play the game

The rules of this game are simple.

Each round, each of you will take turns to ask a "Would you rather" question. You then have to decide which option do you prefer.

For example, "Would you rather sleep with the lights turn on or off?"

If you play this game during a party with a group of friends, each round, another person must answer a question.

An alternative way of playing this game is to turn it into a drinking game. In order to play using this game, you will need at least three people.

The rules remain the same, however, all players have to choose their choice simultaneously. The person who has chosen the least popular option will have to drink. If it is a tie, all players have to drink. If everyone has chosen the same option, nobody has to drink.

1

Would you rather...

to have your partner to try something kinky and new with you in the bedroom

OR

learn a new hobby together with your partner?

4

Would you rather...

touch yourself in front of your partner

OR

watch your partner caresses himself or herself?

5

Would you rather...

have sex in a busy train

OR

in a dirty bathroom?

6

Would you rather...

be kissed all over your body

OR

have French kiss with your lover?

7

Would you rather...

watch porn with your lover

OR

be eavesdropped on during sex?

8

Would you rather...

have foreplay only

OR

have sex only without foreplay?

9

Would you rather...

**have the sex talk with
your lover at night**

OR

have sex through Zoom?

10

Would you rather...

have sex inside a car

OR

have sex secretly in a cinema?

11

Would you rather...

give a hand job in a bus

OR

your partner give a hand job in a bus?

12

Would you rather...

your lover to massage for you sexily with chocolate

OR

your lover to massage for you sexily with honey?

13

Would you rather...

your partner to blindfold you during sex

OR

your significant other to tie you up in bed during sex?

14

Would you rather...

to be addicted to sex and have multiple partners

OR

to be married to a sex addict?

15

Would you rather...

your partner to have a one night stand with your best friend

OR

your partner to have a one night stand with a stranger?

16

Would you rather...

to have anal intercourse only

OR

no intercourse ever again?

17

Would you rather...

your partner do a pole dance for strangers

OR

your partner do a pole dance for friends?

18

Would you rather...

watch your significant
other having sex with
your superior

OR

you have sex with his or
her boss?

19

Would you rather...

have a lover who is never satisfied in bed

OR

a lover who is not good in sex?

20

Would you rather...

have sex with your lover lying in a hot tub

OR

have sex standing in the shower?

21

Would you rather...

to have sexual activity with two other people without your lover

OR

watch your lover engaging in a sexual activity with two other strangers?

22

Would you rather...

use a prop to masturbate in front of your lover

OR

use a prop to masturbate when your lover is not around?

23

Would you rather...

have sexual intercourse when you are drunk

OR

your partner to have sex with you while you are asleep?

24

Would you rather...

your partner used ice cubes to trace over your nipple

OR

used massage oil candle wax to tease you during foreplay?

25

Would you rather...

only have oral sex

OR

only have anal sex?

26

Would you rather...

your partner dislike oral sex

OR

was obsessed with anal sex?

27

Would you rather...

have French Kiss using melted chocolate

OR

French Kiss with your lover using melted marshmallows?

28

Would you rather...

read erotica

OR

watch porn?

29

Would you rather...

**make out with your lover
in extreme cold**

OR

in extreme heat?

30

Would you rather...

your partner to be very quiet during sex

OR

your partner to scream during sex?

31

Would you rather...

be on top

OR

bottom during sex?

32

Would you rather...

have sex with protection

OR

have sex without protection?

33

Would you rather...

make out in the morning

OR

at night?

34

Would you rather...

have amazing sex for 60 seconds

OR

average sex for 15 minutes?

35

Would you rather...

**only make love in the
missionary position**

OR

**only make love in the
doggy-style position?**

36

Would you rather...

lose your sex organs

OR

have more sex organs?

37

Would you rather...

be virgin forever

OR

have sex with your siblings for 1 time?

38

Would you rather...

everyone knew what you are thinking all the time

OR

be able to keep your thoughts to yourself but never be allowed to wear clothes?

39

Would you rather...

date someone smelled like garlic

OR

or tobacco all the time?

40

Would you rather...

never get drunk with your lover

OR

get drunk with your partner every night?

41

Would you rather...

French kiss every person at this party

OR

have a one night stand with one person at this party?

42

Would you rather...

make love only in bed

OR

make love in public places?

43

Would you rather...

wear a sports bra for the rest of your life

OR

never wear a bra again?

44

Would you rather...

spit

OR

swallow your lover's discharge?

45

Would you rather...

rub pasta all over your body

OR

rub ice cream all over your body?

46

Would you rather...

be your lover's first love

OR

your lover's last?

47

Would you rather...

suck your partner's earlobe

OR

suck your partner's toes?

48

Would you rather...

be sexless forever

OR

no emotional
conversations forever?

49

Would you rather...

watch your best friend's sex tape

OR

have your best friend watch yours?

50

Would you rather...

slap your lover's butt in public

OR

have your lover slap your butt in public?

51

Would you rather...

sneeze every time you have orgasm

OR

have orgasm every time you sneeze?

52

Would you rather...

never wear underwear again

OR

never wear bras again?

53

Would you rather...

receive flowers every month

OR

receive diamonds every 3 years?

54

Would you rather...

get a good morning text

OR

a good night text?

55

Would you rather...

cry every time you have orgasm

OR

fart every time you have orgasm?

56

Would you rather...

your sex video circulates online

OR

a video showing you masturbating circulates online?

57

Would you rather...

make love in the kitchen

OR

make love in the bathroom?

58

Would you rather...

scream your ex's name in bed

OR

your significant other scream his or her ex's name in bed?

59

Would you rather...

your lover dirty talks in bed

OR

moans gently during sex?

60

Would you rather...

date someone with an awesome bum

OR

date someone with great breasts or six-packs?

61

Would you rather...

never eat your favourite food again

OR

never have sex again?

62

Would you rather...

be a virgin at 42

OR

**never have sex again
after 42?**

63

Would you rather...

burp every time you kiss your lover

OR

orgasm every time you kiss your lover?

64

Would you rather...

be a lover who is not good in kissing

OR

be a lover who is not good at giving head?

65

Would you rather...

be with a lover who is not good in kissing

OR

be with a lover who is not good at giving head?

66

Would you rather...

have a one night stand with a priest or nun

OR

have a one night stand with someone who is already married

67

Would you rather...

get a lap dance in public

OR

give a lap dance to a stranger privately?

68

Would you rather...

**get horny in
inappropriate situations**

OR

never get horny again?

69

Would you rather...

use sex props every time
you have sex

OR

never use sex props
again?

70

Would you rather...

become a porn star

OR

your lover become a porn star?

71

Would you rather...

eavesdrop on your friends having sex

OR

your friends eavesdrop on you having sex with your lover?

72

Would you rather...

suck a used condom

OR

suck your lover's dirty underwear?

73

Would you rather...

make love in a tent on a campsite

OR

at a hotel balcony?

74

Would you rather...

**make love with your
partner in a library**

OR

**make love with your
partner in a church?**

75

Would you rather...

make love on a beach

OR

make love in a Jacuzzi?

76

Would you rather...

have sex with a sex doll

OR

watch your lover have sex with a sex doll?

77

Would you rather...

have a cosplay sex

OR

be blindfolded during sex?

78

Would you rather...

be caught having sex by a police officer

OR

be caught having sex by your grandparents?

79

Would you rather...

your lover to like BDSM

OR

your lover to like roleplay?

80

Would you rather...

**your lover to be
completely motionless
during sex**

OR

**your lover to be very quiet
during sex?**

81

Would you rather...

have longer foreplay

OR

longer sex?

82

Would you rather...

make love in a public place

OR

make love at your parents' or your lover's parents' house?

83

Would you rather...

make love against the wall

OR

make love on the bed?

84

Would you rather...

**have amazing
conversations**

OR

amazing sex?

85

Would you rather...

go on a month without drinking

OR

go on a month without sex?

86

Would you rather...

cheat on your lover

OR

your partner thought that you have cheated, even though you did not cheat on your partner?

87

Would you rather...

have sex with someone you hate the most

OR

have sex with your ex?

88

Would you rather...

date someone whose hands were always burning hot

OR

date someone whose hands were always freezing cold?

89

Would you rather...

have an amazing body even though you eat a lot

OR

never run out of money?

90

Would you rather...

sleep with a virgin

OR

have sex with someone who has multiple sex partners?

91

Would you rather...

have sex with someone who does not let you to touch her butt

OR

have sex with someone who does not let you to touch her boobs?

92

Would you rather...

have sex with someone with nipple piercings

OR

have sex with someone with clit piercings

93

Would you rather...

work as a stripper

OR

work as a prostitute?

94

Would you rather...

foreplay for an hour every time you had sex

OR

never foreplay again?

95

Would you rather...

have exciting but rough sex

OR

boring sex?

96

Would you rather...

have a small penis but
have stronger orgasms

OR

have a big penis but less
intense orgasms?

97

Would you rather...

your lover bite down your penis

OR

your lover bite down your balls?

98

Would you rather...

make love without kissing
your partner

OR

without using your hands
at all?

99

Would you rather...

keep your shirt on during sex

OR

keep your shoes on during sex?

100

Would you rather...

wait until marriage to have sex

OR

never find your true love?